AF375499

Dedication

For every child who embarks on the delightful journey of 'Joyful Tales of Laughter and Learning,' may the pages be filled with laughter, joy, and the magic of discovery. This book is dedicated to the little ones who inspire us daily to create, learn, and imagine. Your boundless curiosity lights up our world, and this jamboree of adventure is for you.

Acknowledgment

With heartfelt appreciation, I extend my deepest thanks to the incredible individuals who contributed to the creation of 'Joyful Tales of Laughter and Learning.' To the dedicated staff of the schools where I've had the privilege to work, your unwavering commitment to education and the well-being of children has been an inspiration.

To the parents whose trust I've earned over the years as a pediatric occupational therapist, thank you for allowing me to be part of your children's journey. Your support and collaboration have been invaluable.

A special shout-out to my cherished family members who always believed in my storytelling abilities. Your encouragement and enthusiasm fueled the spark that brought this joyful jamboree to life.

May this book be a shared celebration of the joy, learning, and laughter we've experienced together, and may it continue to inspire the young minds who turn their pages.

"I would also like to express my gratitude to OpenAI for their role in helping me articulate certain words in this book"

Samantha the Sock Explorer

Samantha's feet are ready to play,
Join her sock adventure, hooray!
Red or blue, oh, what a choice,
Help her wiggle into cozy joys!"

Jumping Jack and
the Toothbrush Tango

Jumping Jack loves to dance and sway,
Toothbrush tango, let's brush away!
Spin and twirl, teeth so clean,
Jack's dental dance, a shining sheen!"

Tammy's Tummy Tunes

Tammy's tummy, a melody grand,
Healthy foods, oh so grand!
Fruits and veggies, a tasty treat,
Tammy's tunes, a mealtime feat!"

Lily's Lively Loo Routine

Lily's loo routine, a lively dance,
Flushing, washing, a bathroom trance.
Soapy bubbles, giggles too,
Lily's bathroom fun for me and you!"

Oliver's Outdoor Adventure

Oliver's outdoor quest, hats on head,
Sunscreen magic, adventure spread.
Under the sun, a world so wide,
Join Oliver, let's explore outside!"

Mia's Magical Bedtime Ritual

Mia's bedtime, a magical flight,
Teddy bears and stories bright.
Snuggle close, in dreams, we soar,
Mia's bedtime ritual, forevermore!"

Dexter's Dress-Up Derby

Dexter's dress-up derby, oh what to wear,
Clothes galore, let's have a flair.
Stripes or spots, a stylish spree,
Join Dexter's fashion jubilee!"

Penny's Playtime Parade

Penny's playtime parade, toys in a row,
March along, and let your imagination grow.
Giggle, wiggle, toys unite,
Join Penny's playtime, oh, what a sight!"

As our day of fun comes
to an end,
High-fives and giggles
with every friend.
Remember the joy, the
laughter, the cheer,
Until next time, my dear
reader, have no fear!

Whether big or small, young or old,
Adventures await, stories untold.
So close the book, with a chuckle and grin,
Until next time, where new tales begin!"

THE END

JOYFUL CHARACTERS

Samantha the Sock Explorer

Jumping Jack and the Toothbrush Tango

Tammy's Tummy Tunes

Lily's Lively Loo Routine

Oliver's Outdoor Adventure

Mia's Magical Bedtime Ritual

Dexter's Dress-Up Derby

Penny's Playtime Parade

THE GROUP HAVING A SILLY PARTY

THE END

About the Author

Stephen Edakulam is a storyteller and a seasoned pediatric occupational therapist with over 11 years of dedicated experience. Working with babies, high school children, and even adults, Stephen brings a wealth of knowledge and understanding to 'Joyful Tales of Laughter and Learning.'

This enchanting book is a testament to Stephen's commitment to blending the magic of storytelling with the expertise of pediatric occupational therapy, creating a unique and engaging experience for young readers. Join Stephen on a journey that combines laughter, learning, and the joy of imaginative discovery, inspired by years of fostering growth and development in diverse individuals.

More about Stephen

Meet Stephen, a seasoned occupational therapist with over 12 years of dedicated experience, weaving a rich tapestry of care across diverse age groups and unique challenges. Stephen's journey began by specializing in working with children facing severe developmental delays on the spectrum. With unwavering patience, expertise, and boundless compassion, Stephen became a steadfast support for families navigating the intricate landscape of developmental differences.

In the realm of early intervention, Stephen extended expertise to the youngest minds, collaborating with families to nurture and guide babies through crucial developmental milestones. This foundational period became a canvas for Stephen to shape the trajectory of young lives, fostering growth and addressing developmental delays with a gentle touch.

Transitioning into the dynamic environment of an orthopedic clinic, Stephen broadened the scope of occupational therapy, offering rehabilitation services for individuals of all ages recovering from physical trauma. Stephen became a healing presence, guiding each person through the intricacies of recovery and reclaiming independence.

Today, Stephen continues to have a profound impact as an occupational therapist specializing in children, catering to those with special needs and those without. With a commitment to holistic development, Stephen works directly with children and empowers families by creating sensory gyms within their homes. This hands-on approach ensures that therapeutic interventions seamlessly extend into the daily lives of those under Stephen's care.

Beyond the clinical setting, Stephen wears another hat with passion – that of a realtor. As a real estate professional, Stephen helps families find homes, transforming the search for a house into the beginning of a beautiful journey. Stephen is especially passionate about assisting new families and couples with little children to create a beautiful atmosphere in their new homes. For Stephen, finding homes for people is not just a profession but a means to help families create beautiful stories in their new homes.

In Stephen's latest creation, 'Joyful Tales of Laughter and Learning,' children are invited on a delightful journey where simple Activities of Daily Living (ADL) tasks transform into fun and joyful adventures. This book, crafted with the expertise of an occupational therapist and the heart of a realtor, caters to children with special needs and those without, making everyday tasks exciting and engaging.

As Stephen continues to enrich the lives of those touched by the spectrum of occupational therapy and real estate, 'Joyful Tales of Laughter and Learning' stands as a testament to Stephen's dedication to creating laughter, fostering learning, and unlocking the boundless possibilities of growth.

Stephen Edakulam

Contact

For reading engagements comments, or to order bulk copies,
Please reach out to me at any of my Social Media outlets:

Instagram - stephenedakulam

Email- Stephenrealtor87@gmail.com

Sedakula@icloud.com

THE END

9 798869 150882